AFRICA

Cultures and Costumes Series:

- The British Isles
- Oceania
- Africa
- The Middle East
- China and Japan
- Native America
- Greece and Turkey
- France
- Spain and Portugal
- Northern Europe
- Italy and Switzerland
- Eastern Europe
- India and Sri Lanka

AFRICA

CHARLOTTE GREIG

MASON CREST PUBLISHERS

www.masoncrest.com

Mason Crest Publishers Inc.
370 Reed Road
Broomall, PA 19008
(866) MCP-BOOK (toll free)
www.masoncrest.com

First printing 2002

1 2 3 4 5 6 7 8 9 10

Library of Congress Cataloging-in-Publication Data available

ISBN 1-59084-433-5

Printed and bound in Malaysia

Editorial and design by
Amber Books Ltd.
Bradley's Close
74–77 White Lion Street
London N1 9PF

Project Editor: Marie-Claire Muir
Designer: Hawes Design
Picture Research: Lisa Wren

Picture Credits:
All pictures courtesy of Amber Books Ltd, except the following:
Corbis: 30; **Heritage-Images / British Library:** 50.

ACKNOWLEDGMENT
For authenticating this book, the Publishers would like to thank Robert L. Humphrey, Jr., Professor Emeritus of Anthropology, George Washington University, Washington, D.C.

Contents

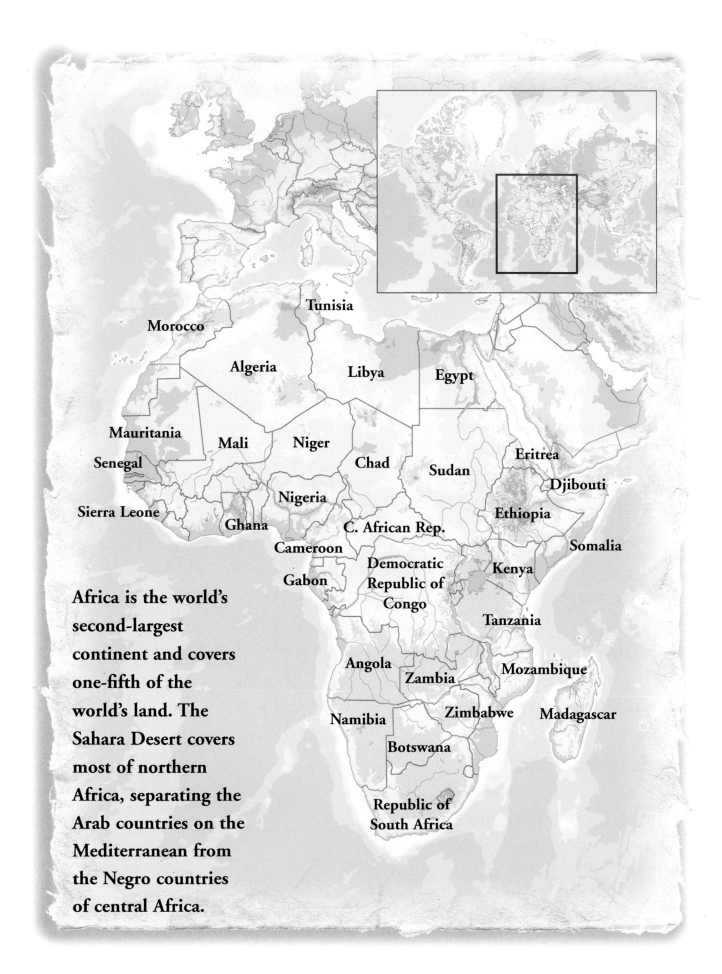

Tunisia

Morocco

Algeria

Libya

Egypt

Mauritania

Mali

Niger

Chad

Sudan

Eritrea

Djibouti

Senegal

Sierra Leone

Nigeria

Ethiopia

Somalia

Ghana

C. African Rep.

Cameroon

Kenya

Gabon

Democratic
Republic of
Congo

Tanzania

Angola

Zambia

Mozambique

Zimbabwe

Madagascar

Namibia

Botswana

Republic of
South Africa

Africa is the world's second-largest continent and covers one-fifth of the world's land. The Sahara Desert covers most of northern Africa, separating the Arab countries on the Mediterranean from the Negro countries of central Africa.

Introduction

Nearly every species in the animal kingdom adapts to changes in the environment. To cope with cold weather, the cat adapts by growing a longer coat of fur, the bear hibernates, and birds migrate to a different climatic zone. Only humans use costume and culture—what they have learned through many generations—to adapt to the environment.

The first humans developed their culture by using spears to hunt the bear, knives and scrapers to skin it, and needles and sinew to turn the hide into a warm coat to insulate their hairless bodies. As time went on, the clothes humans wore became an indicator of cultural and individual differences. Some were clearly developed to be more comfortable in the environment, others were designed for decorative, economic, political, and religious reasons.

Ritual costumes can tell us about the deities, ancestors, and civil and military ranking in a society, while other clothing styles can identify local or national identity. Social class, gender, age, economic status, climate, profession, and political persuasion are also reflected in clothing. Anthropologists have even tied changes in the hemline length of women's dresses to periods of cultural stress or relative calm.

In 13 beautifully illustrated volumes, the *Cultures and Costumes: Symbols of their Period* series explores the remarkable variety of costumes found around the world and through different eras. Each book shows how different societies have clothed themselves, revealing a wealth of diverse and sometimes mystifying explanations. Costume can be used as a social indicator by scientists, artists, cinematographers, historians, and designers—and also provide students with a better understanding of their own and other cultures.

ROBERT L. HUMPHREY, JR., Professor Emeritus of Anthropology,
George Washington University, Washington, D.C.

North Africa

Separated from much of Africa by the huge Sahara Desert, North Africa has developed independently from the rest of the continent. Today, North Africa shows traces of European, Arab, and African cultures, yet it is distinct from all of them.

In Europe, North Africa was regarded as the southernmost part of the Mediterranean and known as Barbary, while the Arabs in the Middle East called it the Maghrib ("the West"). Despite many invasions and foreign influences, over the centuries, it has maintained an independent identity and culture of its own.

The native people of North Africa are the Berbers. Their name comes from the Latin word *barbara*, a term the Romans used to describe any people who were not part of their Empire. The Berbers' own name for their people is Imazighen, meaning "free men." They are thought to have lived there since the second millennium B.C., and throughout their history have found sanctuary from Arab and European colonizers in North Africa's great range, the Atlas Mountains. Today, the Berbers live in the mountains and deserts of Morocco, Algeria, Tunisia, Libya, and Egypt. There are also Berber tribes in Mauritania, Mali, and Niger.

Originally, most Berber tribes were settled farmers who had a structured society with complex marriage and inheritance laws. Between the 7th and 12th

Great palaces such as these were built by the Moors between the 11th and the 13th centuries. Walls were decorated with patterns and words, not with pictures, in accordance with Islamic beliefs.

The tent of a nomadic Arab tribe is shown in this image. Arab women hide their valuables, such as coral beads, necklaces, earrings, and jewels, in a goatskin bag at the foot of the central pole.

centuries, Arabs invaded the area, so the Berbers changed their way of life, becoming **nomads** and moving around the mountains and deserts in search of food. This nomadic way of life continued as various European powers, including France, Spain, and Britain, colonized the area.

Although the Berbers resisted the Arab religion of Islam for many years, eventually most tribes came to accept it. However, even today, aspects of Berber culture remain different from that of the Arabs. For example, Berber women have a good deal of personal freedom. They have property rights and can divorce easily and remarry, unlike many Muslim women.

Bridal Costume

In Morocco, the traditional Berber wedding is a lavish affair. When a bride is engaged to be married, she receives rings, bracelets, and necklaces from her husband-to-be, as well as luxurious cloth, gowns, and perfume. Before the wedding, she takes a special bath in the bridal chamber attended by her maids, who are called the *negassa*. Her face is heavily made up, with white dots on her cheeks and chin, and her hands and feet are decorated with henna, a type of reddish-brown vegetable dye. She is then dressed in richly embroidered robes, some made of gold cloth. The bride also wears a heavy headdress like a crown with gold netting at either side of the face, and large ropes of jewelry around her neck. At her wedding, she is carried on the shoulders of the *negassa*, who later check that the wedding night has gone well before leaving the couple alone.

The *Haik*

Berber men and women, along with many other inhabitants of North Africa, wear the **haik**, a long, white cloth drape. The white *haik* is an echo of the Roman

These Berber women are dressed in their ceremonial clothes: brightly colored patterned robes with fringed edges, enameled jewelry, and coins. Their flat headdresses enable them to carry pots on their heads.

toga, introduced in ancient times when the Romans colonized North Africa. The *haik* is worn in different ways—for example, belted over a simple tunic, or over a caftan. The *haik* is usually made of handwoven, pure white cotton, but in southern Morocco, it is sometimes striped with blue or black.

In addition to the *haik*, Berbers wear the *izar*, a draped piece of cloth of Greek origin, held onto the shoulder with pins. The word *izar* is thought to be an early Arab term for a variety of different Berber wraps known as *a'aban*, *akhusi*, *afaggu*, and *tahaykt*. In Morocco, Jewish women wear a fringed shawl that is known as an *izar*.

In winter, Berber women wear a woolen robe called a *zlazil* to keep warm. For men, an outer robe called a **burnoose** is worn, along with a turban or cap.

The *Djebba*

Another Berber garment that dates from ancient times is the *djebba*. This is a rough shirt with a horizontal slit for the neck, which corresponds to the ancient Roman tunic. The sleeves, made in two parts, are similar to the *dalmatica*, a wide-sleeved tunic of the late Roman era. The lower part of the sleeve is slanting, in a way that recalls Arab styles, and was probably introduced at the time of the Arab conquest of North Africa.

In the Sahara, Berber women wear tresses of false hair made from black wool, decorated with gold discs. Their necklaces, bracelets, and earrings are of coral, amber, and colored glass.

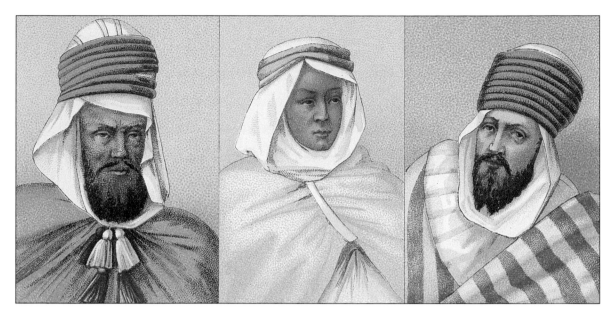

These men wear different styles of turbans and *haiks* (an outer robe). The *haik* is usually white (center), but can also be striped (right) and is fastened in different ways.

Today, Berber men still wear the *djebba* in Morocco. In Algeria, women wear the *dalmatica* as a chemise, or undershirt. Algerian women decorate the *dalmatica* with two colored satin ribbons running over both shoulders, a style that was used in Roman times.

Indigo Veils

The Tuareg are a Berber tribe that inhabits the Sahel, a vast semidesert region fringing the southern Sahara. The Tuareg are often called "the Blue Men" because they dye their clothes with indigo, which often rubs off onto their skin. Unlike Muslim cultures, in which women must veil their faces in front of men, in Tuareg culture, it is the men who must cover their faces in front of women and strangers. Tuareg men wear the indigo-dyed veil as a sign that they have reached manhood, and they wear it even when eating, lifting it briefly to put food into their mouths. The veil also has a practical use in keeping sand out of the eyes and mouth during sandstorms. As more Tuareg people inhabit cities

Berber Jewelry

Berber women's jewelry forms part of their **dowry**. Because the Berbers are primarily a nomadic people who travel around, their valuables have to be in a portable form. For them, jewelry is their money supply. If there is a long drought, the women's jewelry can be traded for animals and other goods.

Berber jewelry features large coins. The coins may be linked in the shape of square collars and worn around the neck, or sewn to head coverings to frame the face. Precious stones are also used. Jewelry consists of earrings, necklaces, anklets, and pins called *bzima*, which are used to hold Berber women's traditional robes together.

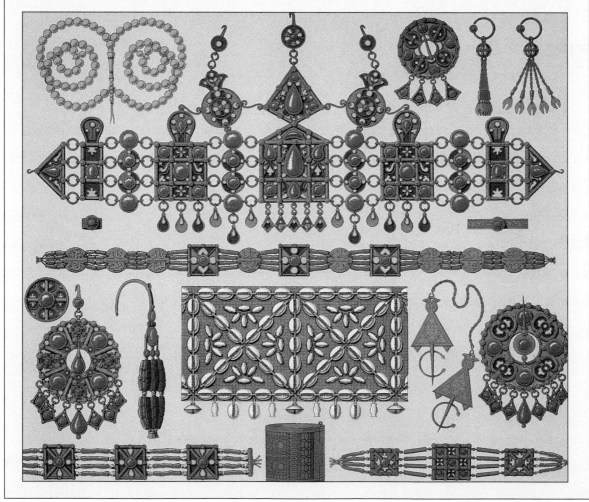

and towns, the veil is worn less often, and today it is often made with **synthetic** dyes that do not rub off on the skin.

Tuareg Jewelry

Today, Tuareg necklaces are sold around the world. The designs are taken from ancient symbols of Berber culture and from the symbols of Islam, brought to North Africa by the Arabs. Among the Tuareg, gold is considered impure, so the necklaces are made in silver and other metals. Many of the designs show crosses; according to Muslim belief, the four points of the cross disperse evil to the four corners of the earth.

Kabyle Culture

The Kabyle are a Berber tribe that lives in Algeria, in a mountainous coastal region that stretches from the Mediterranean Sea to the Grand Kabylie Mountains. The Kabyle have fiercely resisted all attempts at colonization, and

These Berber women wear traditional turbans and coral earrings. The woman in the center wears a round plaque, or *thibeximin*, on her forehead to show that she has a son.

Members of the Kabyle, a Berber tribe who have farmed for centuries, are shown above. The woman second from the left carries a stick to collect olives, while another, far right, gathers figs.

their culture has survived relatively unchanged over centuries. In the 1950s and '60s, the Kabyle fought a long, hard battle against the French in the Algerian war of independence.

Today, tribe members are primarily Muslim, but some are Christian, living in settled villages as farmers, growing olives, figs, and grains, and tending goats. They have a highly structured society in which people belong to different classes, including a servant class. Some types of people—for example, butchers—are kept at a distance and are not allowed to fully take part in the tribe's social life. An assembly of adult men rule each village, and there is a system of law dealing with property and crime. Traditionally, Kabyle men wear the *burnoose,* an outer robe, with a **skullcap** and a straw hat. Women cover their heads with silk scarves and wear striped cotton robes in bright colors.

Bedouin Nomads

In the 12th century, Bedouin tribes from the Arab world invaded the coastal areas of North Africa, and many of the settled Berber tribes changed their way of life. They became nomads like the Bedouins, and began to move around the deserts and mountains in search of food. Today, some desert tribes in Mauritania and other areas show their mixed heritage through their dress; in addition to wearing the classic *haik* and indigo-dyed turbans, they carry a small leather box on a leather string around their necks. Inside the box are verses of Muslim prayers.

The *Mandeel*

Over the centuries, Arab influence on Berber dress has been quite strong. Today, most Berber women wear the half-veil, or *mandeel,* over their mouths when in public. The *mandeel* is usually dark in color and decorated with embroidery at the bottom edge. In addition, Berber women cover their heads with scarves, often in a color that matches their long, plain robes. Like other Arab women, Berber women wear plain outer robes in public; while at home, they wear lighter, finer clothes decorated with embroidery. In the countryside, Berber women often go unveiled.

The *Djellaba*

In Morocco and Algeria, both men and women wear the *djellaba*. This is a long, loose outer garment that is pulled on over the clothes. It has a large hood, big enough to put on over a turban, which has the practical use of keeping the sun off the face and neck. The neck is V-shaped, and the fabric around the neck is often embroidered. For women, there is a clasp at the neck to close the front opening. The *djellaba* usually has full-length sleeves; there are no pockets, but two slits in the side seams enable the wearer to reach the pockets of inner garments. There are variations on the *djellaba* in different areas. For example, in the north it is shorter and more ornate, while in the south it is a smock-like

Medieval Moorish Clothing

The name *Moor* comes from the Latin word *Maurus*, used to describe the inhabitants of the ancient Roman province of Mauritania, which is present-day western Algeria and northeastern Morocco (not to be confused with the modern nearby country of Mauritania). The Moors, of mixed Berber, Arab, and Spanish origin, helped to conquer Spain in the eighth century A.D. From the 11th to the 13th centuries, two great Berber tribes—the Almoravids and the Almohads—built Islamic empires in southern Spain.

The Almoravids wore a *litham*, a face veil that covered the lower half of their faces, as well as the *imama* (turban) and the *burnoose*. The next dynasty, the Almohads, were sober and plain in their dress, criticizing the wearing of gold-laced sandals and ruling that women of all classes should wear the veil. The Almohads wore a type of turban called a *kursiyya*. Under the laws of **ghiyar**, the Almohads decreed that Jews should wear a special costume of yellow turbans and yellow clothes to distinguish them, and until modern times dress codes for Jews continued to be very strict in Morocco.

shirt worn over baggy trousers. For everyday wear, men often wear the *djellaba* over a Western suit or a t-shirt and trousers. Cotton or wool *djellabas* are popular for everyday wear; while for formal events and weddings, they may be made of silk and be heavily embroidered around the neck.

Another typical Moroccan item of dress is the slipper, made of leather and with a flattened heel at the back. Today, many kinds of these slippers, in different styles and decorated with embroidery, are sold in the street markets and shops of Moroccan cities.

Modern Clothing

Today, many ancient styles of Berber and Arab clothing, such as the *haik*, the *djebba*, the *burnoose*, and the *djellaba*, are still worn across North Africa, reflecting the fascinating, complex history of the region. There are also traces of European dress mixed with Berber styles dating from colonial times. Since the 1950s, many Europeans, including French, Spanish, Italian, Greek, and Maltese people, left the country, but echoes of their cultures still remain there. In addition, half a million Jews left North Africa, many of them settling in the newly created state of Israel.

Currently, there is less emphasis on traditional dress in the big cities and coastal areas, but in the deserts and mountains, Berber and Arab tribes continue their ancient crafts, selling goods, such as fabrics, carpets, and jewelry, to tourists and collectors.

A Moroccan street seller wears the traditional *djellaba*. The fabric is striped and edged in white. Today, a variety of styles of *djellaba* are worn over modern Western clothing in Morocco.

The Horn of Africa

The region known as the Horn of Africa has long supported two contrasting cultures. One of these cultures, thriving in geographic isolation, retains its age-old ways. The other, in contact with different peoples through trade, reflects their various influences.

The Horn of Africa is the easternmost projection of the continent, with a curving, pointed shape something like a cow's horn, which is how it got its name. In the countries of Ethiopia, Eritrea, Djibouti, Somalia, and Sudan, two different primary cultures have developed: one Christian and one Muslim. The Christians live in the isolated highlands of Ethiopia, and their culture has, to a large degree, been shielded from foreign influences. Both their style of dress and their jewelry are unique: starkly beautiful, simple, and imaginative. In the coastal regions, centuries of trade with Arab and Indian peoples have created a more diverse material culture. The jewelry and dress of the people here are elaborate and complex, borrowed from many countries.

This illustration shows a collection of Nubian artifacts, including a tent, parasol, weapons, and other equipment. Below, a group of Nubian tribesmen are depicted in traditional dress.

The hot, windy Nubian Desert in the north is home to many nomadic tribes that bring other distinctive cultures to the region. The Rashaida nomads, a Bedouin tribe originally from Saudi Arabia, follows strict Muslim beliefs, which includes veiling the female face and body with the *burga*, a long cloth mask. The Beja, a group of tribes probably of Egyptian ancestry, are famed for their elaborate gold jewelry.

Other peoples of the Horn of Africa include the Harer, with a strongly Arab culture, and the Afar, tough nomads with a primitive but dramatic culture, who inhabit the arid deserts.

Ethiopia

Modern-day Ethiopia is one of the world's poorest countries. Its population is largely rural, and two-thirds of the people are illiterate. Since 1974, when Emperor Haile Selassie was deposed, there has been a great deal of social unrest and conflict in Ethiopia as successive governments, both military and socialist, have failed to bring peace and prosperity to the

This Ethiopian man is dressed for battle in a cotton cloak and leggings. The cloak is held in place with a black panther skin and decorated with red leather edged in silver.

country. In particular, there has been a long and bitter struggle with a neighboring country, Eritrea, which Ethiopia took under its control in 1962. Eritrea finally gained independence from Ethiopia in 1993.

There are two main ethnic groups in Ethiopia: the Amhara and the Oromo. Many other groups, such as the Afar, Tigray, and Saho, also inhabit the country, and many different languages are spoken. Although some of the inhabitants follow the Muslim faith, the majority of the population has been Christian from early times. A small proportion continues to practice a traditional form of **animism**, the belief that certain objects and natural events have souls or conscious life and must be worshipped.

Brocade Umbrellas

In the highlands of Ethiopia, the Amhara people practice one of the most ancient forms of Christianity found in Africa today. For ceremonies, the priests dress in splendid robes, wearing white turbans on their heads. Their cloaks, cut in the shape of a cross, are made of **brocade** silks in brilliant colors. The cloaks are heirlooms handed down from generation to generation. Priests also carry brightly colored, embroidered umbrellas, fringed with gold brocade. The umbrellas are said to symbolize the heavens and the stars.

The Amhara, once known as the Abyssinians, have a centuries-old culture that has developed in isolation from the rest of the world. As early as the fourth century A.D., their ancestors, the Egyptian Copts, were forced to leave their homelands because of persecution for their Christian beliefs, and they settled in Ethiopia. As Islamic invaders came into the country, the Copts were forced to retreat into the highlands, and they lost contact with the Christian world, developing a unique religion and way of life that still survive today.

This separate, austere way of life, which includes many religious observances, such as **fasting**, has made the Amhara the subject of great admiration among many black people around the world, particularly the Rastafarians of the West Indies, who see them as a symbol of black dignity and pride.

The Ethiopian Cross

In Ethiopia, the Christian cross is traditionally crafted in silver and worn as a pendant. Crosses are the most valued item of jewelry in the highlands. In former times, it was possible to tell where a woman was from by the style of her cross; however, today, smiths travel around the country on roads the Italians built in World War II, so the localized styles are less clear.

The crosses were originally cast from wax or cut from Austrian Marie Therese dollars, which was the currency of the country for many years. The designs of the crosses show the influences of several ancient cultures, including those of the Egyptian Copts, the Greeks, the Romans, and the Celts. In the 19th century, silver became more readily available, and more complex openwork designs were made.

In addition to crosses, wide silver bracelets are worn. In the north, there are ornate designs with beads and braided shapes, while in the south, the bracelets are simpler, engraved with plain lines and dots.

The Amhara consider themselves a separate and superior race. They tolerate the Oromo, who are the largest group of people in Ethiopia, but look down on all the Muslim peoples of the coastal region.

The Star of David

The Falashas, a small group of Jewish settlers who live around the ancient city of Gondar, wear the Star of David, fashioned from silver in the same way as the Ethiopian cross. Along with their ancient silver jewelry, Falasha women wear simple robes edged with black embroidery, while the men wear brown **shifts** and white head wraps. Traditionally, the Falashas are craftspeople. Men worked as tanners and weavers, and women as potters and basket makers. Today, as a

Oromo people dress their hair with rancid butter to make it shine. This chief's ivory bracelets are a way of showing that he has defeated many enemies in battle.

result of persecution, many Falashas have migrated to Israel, leaving a small community behind.

Oromo Adornment

The Oromo women in the Ethiopian highlands have a simple, yet elegant style of dress in comparison to the ornate Indian and Arab styles of the lowlanders. Oromo women dress their hair by applying a form of **rancid** butter to give it a sheen. The top part of the hair is braided, and the rest of the hair, which is shoulder-length, is combed free. Often, a silver hair pendant with hanging conical bells is worn. For special occasions, gold-plated combs are worn in the hair.

Other jewelry for women includes long necklaces of triangular and crescent-shaped pendants, which are thought to protect the wearer from evil and from the power of the moon, and small boxes containing **talismans**, or lucky charms, worn around the neck. Women also wear silver beads in the shape of the penis and the breast, which are thought to bring fertility. These fertility symbols are an echo of ancient animist beliefs.

Rashaida Veils

The Rashaida tribe lives in the Nubian Desert of eastern Sudan. They lead a nomadic life, traveling from place to place in tents made of rugs and mats, with herds of camels, which they trade with Egyptians. The women of the tribe are easily recognizable by their distinctive style of dress, which recalls the time of their ancestors, the Bedouin tribes of Saudi Arabia.

As strict Muslims, Rashaida women wear a long veil covering the lower half of their faces. Their bodies are also swathed in long robes. Their style of dress, although modest, is quite flamboyant.

From an early age, Rashaida girls receive an enormous amount of silver jewelry. Their dowry, or bride payment, is also made in jewelry when they marry. They wear many silver bracelets for everyday wear, along with highly decorated veils embroidered in silver thread. Gifts of coins, buttons, and pendants are sewn onto the veil, known as a *burga*, which is restyled every three years. By the time of a girl's marriage, the *burga* is long and highly decorated. In addition to jewelry and veils, Rashaida women wear bright **appliquéd** skirts, giving them a colorful, bold appearance that stands out from the dress of other nomad tribes in the desert.

Rashaida Bridal Costume

A Rashaida bride is covered from head to foot in decorated cloth and jewelry, so much so that her face and body are hardly visible at all. She wears a long silver veil, the *aruse*, which covers her nose and forehead, leaving only two holes for her eyes. The veil across her forehead and around her eyes is edged with gold coins. On her arms are long bracelets, a gift to her from her husband.

Once she is married, the Rashaida woman can take off her long, heavy veil and wear a cotton head cloth, which gives her greater freedom of movement.

Beja Gold

The Beja people, who are thought to be of Egyptian and Arab descent, are the original inhabitants of the desert. They are nomads whose tribes include the Beni Amer and the Hadendawa. Like the Rashaida, the Beni Amer breed and trade camels in the desert. The Hadendawa tend cattle and farmland in the less harsh climate of the Red Sea Hills. These hills are a refuge for the nomadic tribes and are also a source of gold, which in early times was traded with ancient Egypt.

Today, evidence of this history is seen in the dress of Beja women, who wear gold as a way of indicating their status and wealth. Unmarried Beja girls wear gold discs on their foreheads, while married women adorn their faces with gold nose rings and also wear large gold earrings. On their heads, Beja women wear bright muslin head scarves from India, a style that is also popular among Oromo women.

Amber

In addition to silver and gold, amber—polished to bring out its beautiful color—is highly prized as jewelry, and is thought to have supernatural powers. Women wear long amber necklaces, which are often given as wedding gifts. Some of these necklaces, such as the amber and silver *muzé*, a dowry necklace found in Somalia, are very large, with beads as big as stones. Women also wear tight amber **chokers**, which they believe protect the body against chills. Men also value amber as a material for making long prayer-bead necklaces called *tusbah*.

The precious necklaces of the Horn of Africa are made of true amber or copal. True amber is a fossilized resin from conifer trees and is millions of years old; much of it comes from the bed of the Baltic Sea. Copal is also a kind of resin that occurs a few feet below ground, and, like amber, gives off an electric charge when rubbed. Today, false amber from man-made resin, much of it produced in Russia, is often sold to tourists in marketplaces as "Somali amber."

Hadendawa Hairstyles

The Hadendawa are striking people who wear their hair in a huge teased-out style, with mud-caked ringlets hanging down at the back. In their hair, they wear wooden combs and pins that are used for maintaining the style. The Hadendawa are renowned as fighters, and their hairstyles contribute to their fierce image. In the 19th century, their appearance terrified British soldiers in Sudan. Later, the Hadendawa became smugglers at ports on the Red Sea, hiding goods in their hair.

Medieval Harer

The Harer is an ancient city in southeast Ethiopia, close to Somalia. Here, in the foothills of the mountains, the climate is gentler and the land can be farmed. Nomads from Somalia and Oromo tribespeople tend the land and graze their herds outside the city. Arabs established Harer, and it became an important trade center in medieval times. Today, its marketplace is still a bustling meeting place for peoples from all over the region.

Women dominate the jewelry trade in Harer, which is unusual for a Muslim community. According to strict Muslim practice, a woman can be divorced instantly, and must yield her property and possessions, except for her personal jewelry. For this reason, women often collect a large amount of jewelry as insurance, so that they can sell it in case of divorce. In this way, a female-dominated jewelry trade has arisen in Harer, with women buying and selling locally made silver, gold from the Somali coast, and various pieces from India, Iran, and the Arab countries.

Cheap Jewelry

The Afar, a nomadic tribe, lives a frugal life in dome-shaped huts covered with animal skins. The men wear light wraps around their waists and carry knives in their belts. On their feet, they wear tough sandals made of hide. They grow their hair in ringlets and wear necklaces with talismans to bring them good fortune. Known as a warlike people, they also scar their bodies and file their teeth down to points, which increases their fierce appearance.

Afar women wear a wrap of brown cloth, and in the desert, many of them go bare-breasted before marriage. After marriage, they wear a light, black shawl, called a *shash,* over the head and shoulders. The women also wear a lot of bright jewelry, often made from cheap materials, such as nickel and copper, but vivid and striking in its effect. Although they officially follow the Muslim faith, the Afar still hold their own tribal religious beliefs, and much of their jewelry, for both men and women, is designed to ward off evil spirits.

The peoples of the Horn of Africa, ranging from the isolated, proud Amhara highlanders to the tough, fiery Afar nomads of the desert, display a wonderful array of culture and costumes, adorning themselves with a flair and imagination that belie the poverty and harshness that dominate their lives.

This Arab woman (left) wears a flat headdress for carrying objects, and a necklace of sequins decorates her robe. A rich Arab townswoman (right) is dressed in a lightweight veil and *haik.*

East Africa

In East Africa, there are many nomadic tribes with a wide variety of culture and costumes. They move around the country in search of pastures for their herds of cattle. The people have few possessions, but have traditionally placed great value on the beauty of the body, whether male or female.

The tribes of East Africa, known as the Eastern and Western Nilotics, occupy a huge area of land, extending from the swamps of southern Sudan to the Serengeti Plain south of Lake Victoria. Although the different tribes have a wide variety of cultures and costumes, there are some general similarities between them, being mostly tall, physically impressive people with great strength, grace, and agility. As nomads, they use camels and donkeys to carry materials, such as branches and hides for their housing.

Instead of learning to cast metal or carve wood, as more settled peoples often do, these nomadic peoples have directed their creative spirit into adorning their bodies. They wear dramatic jewelry that emphasizes the body's shape, and paint their bodies with mud and minerals of different colors. Some tribes also practice **scarification**, in which a pattern of scars is created on their faces or bodies. In many cases, tribe members go naked except for their jewelry, which gives their appearance added impact.

These proud Masai warriors are in their war dress. The two men on the left are wearing a lion's-mane headdress, which signifies that they have killed a lion. The other warriors both wear an ostrich-feather headdress.

In recent years, governments have tried to impose dress rules on the Nilotic peoples, demanding that they should cover themselves as Western people do. However, research has shown that the way the tribes adorn themselves has a practical use; rubbing their skins with grease, mud, and paint, such as powdered ocher, helps to protect the skin from problems such as **scabies**.

The Nilotic peoples adorn their bodies to look beautiful, but their appearance also has great significance within the tribes, operating as a system of sign language. The jewelry and paint that tribe members wear tell the story of their lives: how old they are, whether single or married, whether approaching puberty or pregnant, whether a grandparent, or in mourning, and so on. In this way, each stage and event in a person's life is marked.

The Lion's-Mane Headdress

Among the Masai, as in other Nilotic tribes, society is ordered by **age sets**. This means that male members of the tribe must pass through three stages of life: as

This tribesman (left) wears a panther skin and necklaces of ivory and shell. A king (right) wears a fur headdress attached with pins. Their hair is dressed with clay and cow dung.

children, as warriors, and as elders. Each of these stages is marked by rituals and by adorning the body according to certain set rules.

During childhood, boys tend the herds of cattle and help their parents with everyday chores. When they reach puberty, they take part in an initiation ceremony in which they are **circumcised**; after this, they become warriors. As warriors, they form a group with other young men of the tribe, and are allowed to roam freely, courting as many girls as they want with songs and dances. After a few years, they become elders and can choose a wife.

This passage to adult responsibility is marked by the dazzling *eunoto* ceremony. To prepare for the ceremony, the warriors gather together and paint their bodies with chalk from limestone cliffs, drawing designs, such as zebra stripes, on themselves. On their heads, they wear the ostrich-feather headdress called *enkurara*. In times gone by, this headdress was worn for war, to make the warrior look tall and imposing, but today, it is only used for ritual wear. If warriors have killed a lion, they are allowed to wear the lion's-mane headdress, called an *oluwaru*. They also wear belts decorated with beads and shells, given to them by their mothers and lovers. During the ceremony, each young man dances and shows off his body paint and headdress until, at the climax of the ceremony, his mother ritually shaves off his hair, which has not been cut since he became a warrior. As she does so, he weeps openly for his lost youth. After the ceremony, an elder wearing a black robe leads him away.

As an elder, the Masai man is dressed in a simple red blanket. His head is greased with ocher and animal fat, and he wears little jewelry. His task is to be a responsible parent, to build up his herds of cattle, and to help tribe members in spiritual matters.

Bead Collars and Earrings

Masai girls wear large, flat, bead collars around their necks. Their hair is kept short to draw attention to these collars, which are made of hundreds of brightly colored beads threaded onto wire and spaced with strips of cowhide. Earrings

A tribesman carries a javelin and a long-stemmed pipe. His loincloth is made of fig leaves and he wears a cotton cap over his braided hair. His bracelets are made of ivory.

worn only on the upper part of their ears shows that they are not married. On their heads, the girls wear bands of beads, often with a pendant in the shape of a stylized bird in the middle of the forehead. Older girls and women wear body wraps, usually a red or brown color; however, sometimes a plaid or printed fabric is acquired, like their beads, through trading. Young girls usually wear only animal hides or belts slung around their waists, and their jewelry and body paint are designed to draw attention to their beauty and grace.

Female circumcision, the cutting out of the girl's clitoris, takes place among many of the tribes in this part of Africa. Shortly before she is married, the Masai girl must undergo this brutal operation. During the six-week period of healing, the girl is instructed by older women about how to behave when she is married. She is not allowed to talk to men, and must be modestly dressed. Her face is painted with white chalk, and she wears a special headband decorated with cowrie shells, which symbolize fertility. At the end of her healing period, her head is ritually shaved in preparation for marriage.

As a married woman, the Masai girl now wears long beaded ear flaps, which she must never take off in front of her husband. Only married women wear blue beads, called *nborro,* in the ear flaps. Her jewelry shows her status as a mother; if she has a circumcised son, she wears pendants called *surutia.* She lends these pendants to him at the *eunoto* ceremony when he becomes an elder.

Butterfly People

The Samburu are a tribe whose young members spend a great deal of their time adorning their bodies and styling their hair. The name Samburu means "butterfly," which well describes the colorful appearance and leisured lifestyle of the warriors, who wear carefully applied face makeup and dye their hair with red ocher. Their hair is lengthened with **sisal** string, and cloth supports are placed under the bangs to make them stand out. Beaded, fringed headbands are also worn to provide shade from the sun. Samburu warriors also wear ivory rings in their ears, giving them a deceptively delicate, feminine look, but, in fact, they are actually strong, brave fighters.

As with the Masai, Samburu girls like to wear a great deal of bead jewelry around their necks. However, the Samburu girls wear loose bead necklaces piled on top of one another instead of flat wire collars. Each necklace is a gift from an admirer, and by the age of 15 or so, the girl hopes to have enough necklaces to pile one on top of another until they reach from shoulder to chin. When she has plenty of necklaces, a Samburu man can propose marriage to her.

Trade Wind Beads

Before the 20th century, most tribes wore jewelry made from shells, animal skins, and animal parts, such as snake bones, giraffe hair, and ivory. Iron was also used. The Masai wore heavy iron necklaces and earrings bought from Swahili blacksmiths on the Kenyan coast, while in southern Sudan, local blacksmiths smelted iron ore to make jewelry. Beads from China and Persia, acquired from Arab and Portuguese traders, were largely used as a form of barter, to exchange for goods, such as cattle and cloth.

At the beginning of the 20th century, mass-produced glass beads began to be imported into Africa in great quantities, since they appealed greatly to the tastes of the tribes. In Sudan, these beads were called "pound beads" because they were sold by the pound; in Kenya, they were called "trade wind beads." The beads soon came to replace the shells and bones tribes used in earlier times.

Nose Pendants

Among the Pokot, young women celebrate their enagaement by wearing large pendants in their noses. These are made of aluminum and are shaped like a leaf. When a girl has been circumcised, she wears brass hoops and coils threaded through holes in her ears. Once she is married, she wears a lip plug.

The Pokot are also renowned for wearing the hair of their ancestors threaded into their own hair. Pokot men's hairstyles are a sign of their status. When they pass into adulthood, the wear a blue skullcap called a *siliop* decorated with feathers. More feathers are added as the man becomes a more important figure in the tribe.

Jewelry from Pots and Pans

In East Africa, tribal jewelry is made from all sorts of common metal objects. The Pokot, the Nuer, and the Dinka wear brass jewelry, such as coiled bracelets, earrings, and lip plugs, made from telephone wire and cartridge cases. Among the Gabbra, the Boran, and the Turkana, aluminum jewelry is made from melting down old cooking pots. The aluminum is made into long, shiny strands of beads for necklaces, bracelets, and arm bands. In the past, some tribes used local iron ore to make their jewelry; today, they prefer to use aluminum, finding it an easier metal to work with.

Spear Dowries

The Azande, who are also called the Niam-Niam, live in the savannah and rain-forest areas of the Sudan, Zaire, and the Central African Republic. They are renowned as ironsmiths, and for a marriage dowry, the groom's family will give 20 spears to the bride's family. The Azande traditionally practice **polygamy**, in which men are allowed to have more than one wife. In the past, important old men of the tribe had so many wives that it was difficult for the young men to find a woman available for marriage.

The Rendille

Like other Nilotic peoples, the Rendille have a complex system of body adornment and hairstyles to show their status in life. The Rendille grandmother wears a wide horsehair collar bound with strips of cloth dyed with ocher (in past years, when elephants were more numerous, this would have been made of elephant-tail hair). Mothers show that they have produced a firstborn son by styling their hair in a **coxcomb**. The coxcomb is made from animal fat, mud, and ocher and is constantly maintained and repaired until the son is

The Azande headdress is made of straw decorated with feathers, and is only worn by men. Azande weapons include the *troumbache*, a saber with a curved blade.

circumcised, at which point the mother shaves her head. She also moves her coiled armbands from below her elbows to her upper arms.

Calf Love

The Dinka people, who have settled in the swampy area of southern Sudan, are among the better-off of the Nilotic tribes. They have a relatively leisured lifestyle, tending to their huge herds of cattle, which they love dearly and celebrate with many rituals. Dinka women and children spend many hours threading beads for **bodices** and jewelry. The men pass the time by dressing their hair, a process that involves bleaching it with a mixture of ash and cow's urine, before creating elaborate styles with caked mud.

When a Dinka boy comes of age, he is given a young calf as a companion. The Dinka identifies closely with his calf, hanging cow's-tail tassels from its horns, just as he decorates his own ivory bracelets with these tassels. He also

The Nilotic men decorate their braided hair with rodent's teeth. The man on the left carries a *troumbache*, a saber with many curved blades. The loincloth worn by the woman (right) is decorated with shells and pieces of glass. Both men and women grease their bodies with ocher.

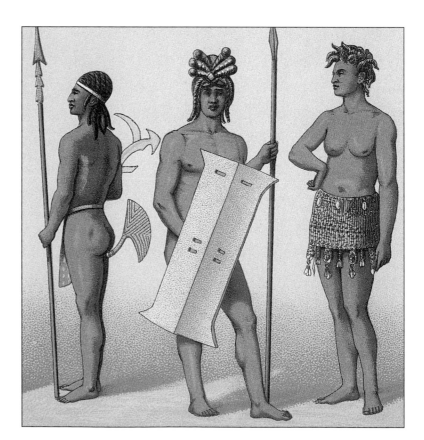

wears a necklace made in the shape of horns. Deep horn-shaped cuts are made in his forehead, a painful process of scarification that he is expected to undergo bravely. This pattern of scars marks him out as a man.

Dinka Corsets

Dinka men wear tight **corsets** made with beads of different colors, which are a sign of their age and marital status. Men from the age of 15 up to 25 wear red and black corsets, while those from the age of 25 to 30 wear pink and purple corsets; those who are over 30 years old wear yellow corsets. Men also wear ivory armbands to show their wealth.

At the age of 17, Dinka girls are fattened up in preparation for marriage. They wear beads in specific patterns that identify their families' status, as well as cowrie shells, which are a sign of fertility. Dinka girls also wear beautiful bodices made of strands of beads that are looped to a central piece, which is designed to show off their bodies. Additional adornments include metal necklaces and belts in pointed triangular shapes.

Traditionally, nothing else is worn with these corsets and bodices, although today, the authorities have ruled that covering clothing should be worn, especially in towns. However, in rural areas, the dignity and grace of the Nilotic peoples, with their naked, adorned bodies, are still an impressive part of the culture of East Africa.

Lip Plates

One painful form of body adornment is that of wearing lip plates, in which the lower lip is stretched out to an extreme degree. This practice is said to have originated in the 19th century to stop slave traders from taking African women, whom they would think ugly with such large, protruding lips.

Whatever the cause, older women among tribes, such as the Kichepo, still wear these plates, never removing them in front of strangers. Today, younger women of the tribe refuse to wear the plates.

West and Central Africa

From Senegal to Cameroon, a wonderful array of costume and headwear changes constantly as foreign influences and new fashions reach the area. Yet despite frequent changes in West African culture and costume, some basic styles have remained the same over centuries.

Across the countries of West Africa, the taste of the people for vibrant colors and striking patterns is catered to by factories that print fabric for sale in the many town markets. West African cloth is often made to commemorate special events or to mark a political campaign, using slogans and images of royalty or politicians. In countries that may lack televisions and books, clothing functions as an effective means of celebrating events in national life.

High Head Wraps

The women of West Africa are renowned for the high, dramatic head wraps they wear, which are draped and tied in simple but beautiful styles, often with

For centuries, men and women from Senegal (upper left) have worn high turbans in colorful fabrics. A West African tribesman (lower left) wears a *gandoura* with an amulet around the neck.

41

This woman wears a head wrap in a contrasting fabric to her body wrap and loose blouse. West African women often wear tall head wraps and accentuate them with large hoop earrings.

a knot on the side of the head and flaring ends to the fabric. With these head wraps, women wear full-length skirt wraps, often in a contrasting color and pattern. A loose blouse with a **yoke** and elbow-length or short sleeves is also worn. Sometimes, the wraps are draped over the upper part of body as well, showing only part of the blouse underneath. Gold earrings and decorated sandals complete the look.

The *Gandoura*

The traditional costume for men in West Africa is a billowing robe called the *gandoura*. This consists of a long piece of cloth with a neck opening, reaching to below the knees at back and front. The sides of the garment are usually left open under the arms and sewn together near the bottom; sometimes, the robe is left open all the way down. The robe has different names in different countries; for example, it is called the *gandoura* or *leppi* in Cameroon, the *agbada* or *riga* in Nigeria, and the *fugu* in Ghana. Under the robe, the man wears a pair of loose, short trousers or Western-style clothing. A variety of headgear may be worn with the robe, ranging from turbans to skullcaps.

Patterns and Designs

West African markets sell three main types of cloth. The first is modern cloth woven and printed in factories, which is often used for making Western-style clothing, but can also be made into traditional African garments for men and women. The second is trade cloth from Java imported by the Dutch. This cloth features batik and *ikat* patterns; batik is made by using a dying method in which certain parts of the cloth are waxed to resist the dye, while *ikat* consists of dyed threads woven to make subtle patterns. (For more information, see pages 53–55 of *Oceania*). Some Javanese-style fabrics are now produced in Africa, but the best-quality ones are imported. The third type of cloth is called country cloth; this cloth is produced by local craftspeople, using ancient methods and designs.

Country Cloth

Lappa cloth is made from strips of cloth woven on a narrow loom, usually by men. The strips are then stitched together in different ways to create a variety of decorative effects. *Garri* cloth, which is made in Sierra Leone, uses a wax-resistant method similar to batik, and the *adire* cloth of Nigeria follows a similar procedure. Making *adire* cloth also involves a type of *ikat* technique. In Cameroon, women of the Bamoun and Bamileke peoples make a blue and white cloth with animal designs on it, called *ndop*. It is produced by sewing raffia shapes over a plain fabric before dyeing it; when the raffia is taken off, the animal shapes show up in white.

Adinkra cloth of Ghana features traditional abstract designs and is usually made by women of the Asante people. However, the most famous Ghanaian cloth is called *kente*. Traditional legend has it that a young man and his friend from Bonwire (now the center of the *kente* weaving trade) learned how to weave by imitating a spider spinning its web. They spun a strip of fabric from raffia and took it to their chief; this *kente* cloth was then adopted as a royal cloth and used for special ceremonial occasions. Today, *kente* cloth is worn for everyday use in Ghana and many other West African countries, and the highest-quality cloth, called *nsaduaso*, which has beautiful silk inlay patterns, is made only for special commissions.

Colors of Life

Today, *kente* cloth is produced across West Africa by many different peoples. Among the Asante of Ghana, colors have special meanings. Yellow, the color of egg yolk and many types of ripe fruit, is associated with fertility; red, the color of blood, symbolizes struggle, sacrifice, and mourning; and blue, the color of the sky, means spiritual harmony, love, and peace. Green, as in many cultures, is the color of new life, of growth, health, and prosperity. Silver, the color of the moon, represents the female essence of life and is worn by women in the form

Timbuktu: City of the Desert

The city of Timbuktu (or Tombouktou) has a fascinating history as a trading center and also, from the 15th century, as a center of Islamic religion. The Tuareg, a tribe of nomads who are a branch of the Berber people, founded it. A remote place situated on the edge of the Sahara Desert, it was important in ancient times as a stopping place for caravans of camels and traders crossing the desert. In the 13th century, it came under the control of the Mali empire and later became a center for the trading of gold, salt, and slaves. Muslim scholars settled there in the 14th century and established the city as a place of legal and moral learning.

In the 16th century, Timbuktu was repeatedly attacked and conquered by desert tribes and began to decline as a focus of civilized life. Today, it is part of Mali.

The nomadic Tuareg tribe founded the city of Timbuktu. They are renowned for their indigo-dyed turbans and veils, which has earned them the name "blue men" of the desert.

of ornaments and jewelry for marriage and other ceremonies. Gold, because it is a precious metal, has the universal association with wealth, high status, and supreme quality.

White and black have special meanings, too. White, the color of ghosts, symbolizes contact with ancestral spirits, while black takes its meaning from the way fruit darkens as it matures. Among the Akan of Ghana, men seek to increase their spiritual power by blackening their walking sticks, known as "knobkerries," which are symbols of their status in society.

Turbans and Robes

The inhabitants of Mali are divided into "white" and "black" populations. The "white" people are those of Arab and Berber descent, who live primarily in the Sahel region. Islamic codes of dress—for example, the covering of women's bodies and the veiling of their faces—still persist here, although in some areas, women do not wear the veil. For men, Arabic turbans and robes are commonly worn. Tuareg men are particularly recognizable by their indigo-dyed, dark-blue clothing and the glittering indigo veil they always wear over the lower half of their faces.

Fulani Beauty Parades

The Fulani are a tribe that can be found all over West Africa, primarily in Mali, Nigeria, Cameroon, Senegal, and Niger. Originally, they were a **pastoral** people who herded cattle, but over the centuries, they adopted other ways of life, settling on the land and farming, or working in towns. Many of the tribes' different branches have adopted the Islamic faith, especially those living in urban areas. In Nigeria and Niger, the Fulani established themselves as rulers of an Islamic empire, taking over the language and culture of the largest ethnic group there, the Hausa.

Although many urban Fulani peoples have absorbed other cultures and ways of life, the pastoral tribes still follow their ancient beliefs, ways of life, and style of dress. One branch of the Fulani, the Wodaabe, has refused to accept Islam and still holds to its traditional animist religion, worshipping the spirits of nature and natural objects. They move around the country with few possessions, carrying their goods on camels or donkeys and storing food and other items in dried gourds.

Among the Wodaabe tribe, each stage of life is celebrated with special ceremonies; for example, there is a ceremony in which husbands-to-be dance to display their beauty to the young girls of the tribe, showing themselves ready to be selected by a bride. In preparation for the ceremony, the young men will spend hours making up their faces with a pale yellow powder, then applying colors and patterns that will show off the whites of their eyes and their teeth. During the ceremony, they will bare their teeth, roll their eyes, and then make strange grimaces. For the beauty parade, the men wear feminine, tightly wrapped skirts, feathers, and beads, shaving their foreheads and painting their faces with red ocher.

The unmarried girls are less elaborately dressed and wear only a skirt wrap to show their unmarried status. They also braid their hair in certain styles to show their status in the tribe. They watch the boys dance and choose their husbands-to-be on the basis of how beautiful and virile they are.

The "Witch Doctor"

Today, Gabon is one of the wealthier countries of West Africa, being rich in oil and mineral reserves and having a small population. Gabon achieved independence in 1960 after years of rule by France, during which time most of the country's inhabitants adopted the Christian faith. However, in the rainforests and savannah regions of the country, some tribes still continue a traditional way of life. Animist religions, in which nature and natural objects are worshipped, still persist, presided over by spiritual healers. From the 18th century,

In Gabon, the "witch doctor" traditionally wears a loincloth with a belt of white beads, fringed with red chenille. Around his neck, he wears strings of large colored beads.

Europeans called these African religious advisers "witch doctors," a term that has misleading associations with European ideas of black magic.

Ghost Masks

The Mpongwe tribe, which belongs to the Ogowe people, is small in number, but it has played an important part in Gabon's development. Their culture is renowned for its complex death rituals, for which people make "ghost masks" to represent dead female ancestors. Among the Mpongwe, death is seen as a pathway to the ancestors, bringing the dead person closer to loved ones who have already died.

In order to celebrate this transition, a male dancer appears at dawn or dusk, wearing the ghost mask and dressed in a costume of woven raffia, which hangs

These women of the Mpongwe tribe are in traditional clothing. Wide pants (left) or a skirt wrap (right) are worn with a cloak over the shoulders, leaving the chest bare. The hair is often braided into a pointed style (right)

Mpongwe woman wear strings of carefully chosen beads to decorate their bare chests. They often attach a *moondah*, an ornament such as a tiger's claw, to the necklaces. This woman's garment is also decorated with a patterned motif around the bottom.

from his neck to his feet, completely covering his body. He balances himself on stilts, which may be more than 10 feet (3 m) high, and he dances through the town, performing acrobatic tricks while chants are sung.

The death masks often show the woman's face with traditional scarification marks in the middle of the forehead and between the eyebrows. Scarification is a process whereby the skin is wounded so that raised scars develop. These scars heal into a permanent pattern of marks. The masks also show a variety of hairstyles popular among the Mpongwe women, including braids that are piled high on the head to form a peak at the top, a style that denotes femininity. The face of the mask is painted white with **kaolin**, a substance that is thought to contain great power.

Today, across West Africa, tribal culture gives rise to a huge variety of vivid clothing, jewelry, and body adornment, both in modern fashions and in ancient traditional costumes.

South Africa

From the 17th century, South Africa's black population has been augmented by white Europeans and Asians, culminating in a strict segregation policy called apartheid, under which many aspects of tribal culture declined. Today, with apartheid abolished, the country's distinctive native heritage has a chance to revive.

The countries of southern Africa are home to peoples from many ethnic backgrounds. In South Africa, the majority of the population is made up of black Africans, including the Xhosa, the Zulu, the Swazi, the Ndebele, the Sotho, the Pedi, and the Tswana. The rest of the population is made up of mixed-raced peoples of Malay and Indian descent, called "coloreds," and white people of European descent.

In 1652, Jan van Riebeeck, a Dutchman, established a colony at the Cape of Good Hope as a trading post for ships from the Dutch East India Company. These Dutch settlers were known as Boers and later, as Afrikaners. The mixing of the Afrikaners with native peoples, such as the Khoikhoin, whom the Dutch called the Hottentots, resulted in a group of mixed-race people known as "Cape coloreds." In the century that followed, the Afrikaners moved inland, farming in the territories of the Xhosa people, with whom there were many conflicts. In

The shield and the strips of animal fur tied around the man's arms and legs identify him as a Zulu warrior. Today, his traditional costume is reserved for special ceremonies, such as weddings.

1765, the British captured the Cape. After a long struggle with the Afrikaners, the British gained control in 1902. South Africa achieved independence in 1934, and in 1948, the Afrikaner-dominated National Party introduced a system of **apartheid** in which the population was divided into ethnic groups. Whites had most of the economic and political power, blacks had virtually no rights at all, and in between were the "coloreds." Apartheid ended in 1994, when South Africa held its first all-race democratic elections and Nelson Mandela became the first black president.

Panther Skins

The system of apartheid meant that, for many years, the tribal way of life and culture of black South African peoples was suppressed. In particular, native tribes, such as the Khoikhoin (Hottentots) and the San (Bushmen), were reduced to small numbers by colonial wars, disease, and poverty.

Before the arrival of the Dutch in South Africa, these tribes were thriving with a pastoral way of life, moving around the country with their herds of animals. The Khoikhoin wore clothes made of animal skin, such as panther, with the fur worn against the skin. They also dyed the skins in various colors. Both men and women adorned themselves with long feather headdresses and necklaces with large metal pendants, and they pierced their ears with bone ornaments.

Today, small numbers of the Khoikhoin live on reserves or among Europeans in South Africa and neighboring Namibia. They have adopted a primarily Western way of life, but a few still follow the traditional pastoral ways of life.

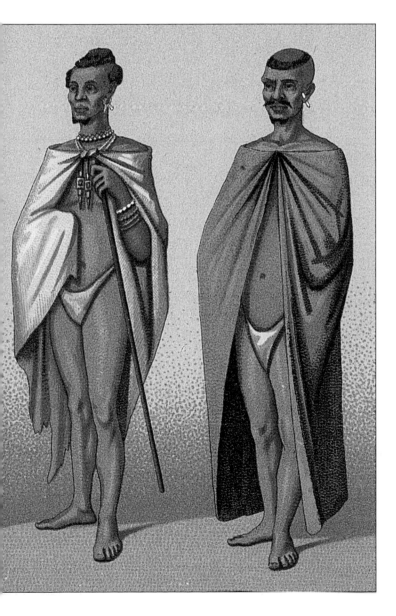

These South African tribesmen wear animal skin loincloths with the fur worn against the skin. Their shields and *assegais* (spears) are also made of animal skin. For hunting, leather sandals are worn.

This Zulu chief wears a leopard skin on his chest and animal fur around his wrists and knees, indicating his status. His headdress is made of otter skin and vulture feathers.

Zulu Warriors

The Zulus are the largest black ethnic group in South Africa. Before the 19th century, they grew crops and herded cattle in the grassland areas of the region. In the early 19th century, they fiercely resisted the Europeans' attempt to take away their lands and resources, forming a Zulu empire with neighboring Nguni peoples under their leader Shaka. However, they eventually lost their independence, and today, most rural Zulu people earn a living as laborers on farms, or working in South Africa's big cities.

Despite the decline in their status, the Zulus remain a proud people with a wide knowledge of their history and culture. Traditional Zulu society is organized in a **patriarchal** way, in which the authority of fathers and husbands

The Hottentot Venus

The exotic appearance of the Khoikhoin caused great excitement among the Europeans, who had never seen such people before. In 1810, a British ship's doctor named William Dunlop noticed the unusually large shape of one Khoikhoin woman, whose Afrikaans name was Sara Baartman. He took her to London and exhibited her as a freak of nature and a scientific curiosity. She was made to perform tricks for the public, showing off her body. In 1814, she was sold to a French entrepreneur, who exhibited her in Paris as the "Hottentot Venus." Later, Sara Baartman became an alcoholic and a prostitute and died when only 27 years old. Her sexual organs and brain were preserved and displayed in Paris until 1985. Recently, her remains were returned to the South African government in a gesture of apology for her cruel treatment at the hands of the colonial Europeans.

Shields and Spears

For ceremonies, warriors traditionally carry bold, dramatic shields in an oblong shape, curved into a point at either end. The shields feature oblong slits in two rows down the middle. *Assegais* (spears) and knobkerries (walking sticks) are also carried. On their legs and arms, the Zulu warrior ties strips of lion's mane, which mark him as a hunter. Chiefs wear leopard-skin cloaks to distinguish them as leaders; a variety of other skins are also used, such as buffalo and otter. Zulu ornaments made of ivory and skin, such as necklaces, bracelets, and headbands, indicate the wearer's age group and status within the tribe; for example, chief counselors are allowed to wear a leopard-skin headband.

is paramount. The Zulu man is allowed several wives, who are ranked in order of importance. The "great wife" is the most senior, being the mother of the man's heir. When a man dies, his wife is expected to marry her husband's brother.

Among the Zulus, military traditions were once strong. The young men were initiated into age sets, groups of warriors who lived and worked together away from their families. Each age set became a unit of the Zulu army, controlled by the king. The men from an age set, or regiment, could only marry when the king gave them permission. The king was also responsible for the nation's spiritual well-being, performing rain-making and other ceremonies in accordance with the Zulus' religious beliefs. The Zulus believed in a creator god as well as in evil spirits, ideas that later became mixed with Christianity.

As colonial power increased, the importance of the Zulu kings, chiefs, and military traditions declined. Traditional Zulu war costume is now worn only for weddings and other ceremonies.

The *Danga*

The Xhosa are another Nguni tribe whose homelands are mostly in the Eastern Cape province of South Africa. They were once known as *kaffirs,* a derogatory Afrikaans term for black people, and they fought a long battle against European settlers to retain their lands, which they called *Ciskei.* The Europeans eventually conquered the Xhosa and named the land Transkei. In 1959, the government designated Transkei as a separate area for the Xhosa people, and afterward the region suffered economically. Many Xhosa men have left to seek work elsewhere in the country. In 1994, when apartheid came to an end, Transkei became part of Eastern Cape province, but by then, the Xhosa way of life and culture were fragmented.

Like the Zulu, the Xhosa are farmers and cattle herders, with a strong patriarchal culture led by a chief tribesman and a council of men from smaller clans. Their tribal dress is now seen primarily at special events and ceremonies. Traditional costume includes a long turquoise necklace reaching to the waist, called a *danga*, which is worn by both men and women. The men also wear goatskin bags made by pulling the animal's body out of its skin in such a way that the skin remains whole.

Young Xhosa girls wear a short, plain skirt and go bare-breasted. They also wear head cloths as a mark of respect to older tribe members. Girls of marriageable age wear longer skirts and turbans; married women are expected to cover their breasts and wear a bigger head wrap. The bigger and more elaborate the head wrap, the higher the woman's status in the tribe.

Ndebele Beadwork

The Ndebele, another Nguni people, are renowned for their beautiful beadwork, which is quite different in style from that of the other tribes of South Africa. In the 16th century, Portuguese traders first brought glass beads to the region, and since then, the Ndebele have used beads in brilliant, geometric designs to decorate their traditional costumes.

Ndebele girls wear thick cords around their waists, from which hang small beaded aprons. Boys wear small loincloths made of goatskin. As the girls get older, the apron becomes bigger, until they reach marriageable age. At this age, they replace their soft aprons with stiff, boarded ones, which were traditionally made of dried skin, but are now made of cardboard and canvas. They are covered with beaded patterns in many colors.

More beads make up the Ndebele girl's large neck collar. Today, these collars are often cut and laced up at the back, so that Ndebele schoolgirls can bend their heads to read and write. When she marries, the Ndebele girl wears an even bigger collar, called a *rholwani,* made of twisted grass and beads. Above this, several tight copper bands are worn around the neck; copper bands also adorn her arms and legs. In addition to wearing the *rholwani,* married women also cover their shoulders and their heads; to do this, they wear imported striped blankets and headbands of beads in many different styles.

For males, there are few rules about clothing until the age of circumcision, when they have to wear an apron beaded in geometric designs. For ceremonies, the men carry round cowhide shields with thin sticks attached to the inside to make a handle; the sticks also make a rattling noise in battle.

This Ndebele woman wears a finely worked bead headdress in a traditional style, along with bead necklaces, bracelets and anklets. Her only other clothing is a short skirt.

Knobkerries and spears are carried as part of the full traditional regalia. In the past, fur and leather shoulder capes and headdresses were worn, but these are not often seen now.

Tribal Revival

Other ethnic groups of South Africa, such as Cape Malays, have their own styles of dress. The Cape Malays are a Muslim minority who live in separate communities and adopt many aspects of Islamic dress. The so-called "coloreds," who mostly live in and around Cape Town, are ethnically mixed. Under the apartheid system, in which people were segregated according to their racial backgrounds, the "coloreds" were forbidden to marry into other racial groups, and many of their political rights were abolished. In this way, they came to form a separate social group of their own.

Today, most "coloreds" wear Western dress, along with white and black South Africans. However, since the end of apartheid in South Africa, there has been an effort to revive the traditional dress of the different communities, especially of the many black tribal groups. The great variety of cultures and wealth of exotic costumes are a heritage that many South Africans today regard with pride, and seek to reestablish in all the countries of southern Africa.

Glossary

Note: Specialized words relating to clothing are explained within the text, but those that appear more than once are listed below for easy reference.

Age set a group of tribe members divided by age and stage in life instead of by family membership

Animism the belief that natural objects and events, such as sky and rainfall, have souls and must be worshipped

Apartheid a system adopted in South Africa whereby people were divided into separate groups on the basis of their ethnic backgrounds

Appliqué a cutout decoration fastened to a larger piece of fabric

Bodice the upper part of a dress

Brocade a fabric characterized by raised designs

Burnoose A long outer robe made of cotton or wool, covering most of the body

Choker a collar or necklace worn closely around the throat or neck

Circumcision a process whereby the foreskin of a boy's penis is removed; in Africa, some tribes practice female circumcision, in which the girl's clitoris is cut out

Coxcomb an ostentatiously conceited man

Dowry goods, property, or money offered for a bride, or given with the bride at marriage

Ghiyar meaning "unbeliever," it is the name given to the laws outlining the dress regulations for those not belonging to Islam

Fast (v.) to go without food for a period of time

Haik an outer garment of cotton, wool, or silk, usually white but sometimes dyed and striped, thought to have developed from the Roman toga

Kaolin fine, usually white clay used in ceramics

Nomad someone who moves around the country in search of food, hunting animals and gathering wild food

Pastoral relating to a tribe whose way of life revolves around grazing cattle on pastures

Patriarchal relating to a society in which the authority of the male is supreme

Polygamy a practice whereby a man takes two or more wives

Rancid having an unpleasant smell or taste

Scabies contagious itch caused by parasitic mites

Scarification a type of body adornment used in Africa and elsewhere, in which wounds are made in the skin in such a way that they heal to form a pattern of scars

Shift (n.) a loose fitting or semifitted dress

Sisal a strong, durable white fiber used especially for hard-fiber cordage and twine

Skullcap a close-fitting cap

Synthetic relating to something produced artificially

Talisman a small object, such as a carved stone, believed to protect the wearer from harm

Yoke a fitted or shaped piece at the top of a skirt or at the shoulder of various garments

Timeline

3200 B.C.	Weaving industry begins in Africa.
500	The Meroe empire, ruled by the Ethiopian or Cushite dynasty, flourishes in Africa.
A.D. 300	Christianity is introduced to Ethiopia.
600	Arab invasion of North Africa.
700	Muslim conquest of Spain.
1000	Almoravids and later Almohads build Islamic empire in Spain and North Africa.
1100	Bedouin Arabs invade North Africa; Berbers become nomads.
1238	Work begins on the building of the Moorish Alhambra palace at Granada, southern Spain.

1500	West African slave trade begins.
1652	Jan van Riebeeck founds a colony at the Cape of Good Hope.
1795	British forces capture the Cape, South Africa.
1813	King Sahle Selassie rules Ethiopia.
1814	The "Hottentot Venus" is exhibited in Paris as a freak of nature.
1868	Discovery of gold, and later, diamonds in South Africa.
1880	French pacify Berbers in North Africa.
1902	Boer resistance to British colonists in South Africa is destroyed.
1930	King Haile Selassie rules Ethiopia.
1935	Italy invades and occupies Ethiopia until 1941.
1948	The white National Party introduces apartheid into South Africa, separating people on the basis of their ethnic backgrounds.
1948	Kenya census shows population doubling every 30 years; population explosion continues until 1984.
1950	Libya and Algeria begin to export large quantities of oil.
1950	European population of North Africa reaches a peak of nearly two million, then declines as many Europeans, including Jews, leave the region.
1960	Gabon declares independence.
1962	Ethiopia takes control of Eritrea.
1963	Kenya achieves independence.
1966	Lesotho and Botswana become independent.
1967	South West Africa renamed Namibia.
1974	Swahili becomes the official language of Kenya; Ethiopia's Marxist regime, the Derg, deposes King Haile Selassie.
1993	Eritrea achieves independence.
1994	South Africa establishes an all-race democracy under Nelson Mandela.
1995	Federal government system is established in Ethiopia.

Online Sources

www.bikeabout.org
A traveler's account of traditional Moroccan clothing, including the *djellaba*.

www.costumes.org
A general site on costumes; go to "ethnic" and then to "Africa" for information and photographs on African costumes, including modern-day national dress.

www.falasha-recordings.co.uk
History and culture of the Falasha people of Ethiopia.

www.frif.com
Information on the Hottentot Venus from filmmaker Zola Maseko.

www.kenzi.com
Photographs and information on the Tuareg indigo veil or *shesh*.

www.natachascafe.com
Photographs and information on Tuareg necklaces.

www.peopleteams.org/amhara
Up-to-date report on the Amhara people of Ethiopia.

www.twooceans.co.za
Photographs and information on the Ndebele tribespeople.

http://webuscrs.anct-chi.com
Useful information on West African *kente* cloth, giving historical background and details of production techniques, spiritual symbolism, and how to wear the cloth.

www.wsu.edu:8080
History of Timbuktu and the Mali empire.

Further Reading

Capald, Gina. *African Customs: Costumes, Legend, and Lore*. Torance, CA: Good Apple, 2001.

Fisher, Angela. *Africa Adorned*. New York: Abrams, 1984.

Kennett, Frances. *World Dress: A Comprehensive Guide to the Folk Costume of the World*. London: Mitchell Beazley, 1994.

Lynch, Annette. *Dress, Gender, and Cultural Change: Asian American and African American Rites of Passage*. New York: Berg Publishing Ltd, 2000.

Mattet, Lawrence. *Arts and Cultures 2002: Antiquity, Africa, Oceania, Asia, Americas 1977–2002*. Paris, France: Vilo Publishers, 2002.

Picton, John. *Art of African Textiles: Technology, Tradition and Lurex*. London: Barbican Art Gallery: Lund Humphries Pub. Ltd., 1995.

Ross, Doran H. *Wrapped in Pride: Ghanaian, Kente and African American Identity (UCLA Fowler Museum of Cultural History Textile Series No. 2)*. Los Angeles, CA: University of California, Museum of., 1998.

The Author

Charlotte Greig is a writer, broadcaster, and journalist. She has written on culture, literature, music, and history. She is the author of several books, and has written, researched, and presented programs for BBC Radio 4, and has contributed articles to national newspapers, *The Guardian* and *The Independent*. She has an MA in Intellectual History from Sussex University.

Index